Kate Lamont

# Celebrating

Kate Lamont

Thanks to all my kitchen staff and Jenny Foreman
for their cheerful and patient assistance.
And to my sister, best friend and fiercest critic.

# Celebrating

## Kate Lamont

FREMANTLE
PRESS
fine independent publishing

First published 2001 by
FREMANTLE ARTS CENTRE PRESS
PO Box 158, North Fremantle
Western Australia 6159.
www.facp.iinet.net.au

New expanded edition, 2007
Copyright text © Kate Lamont, 2001 and 2007.
Copyright photographs © Leon Bird, 2001 and 2007.

Consulting Editor Cate Sutherland.
Designer Margaret Whiskin
Printed by Everbest Printing Company, China.

Lamont, Kate, 1962- .
        Celebrating.

        New expanded ed.
        Includes index.
        ISBN 9781921361005 (pbk.).

        1. Cookery. I. Title.

        641.5

# Contents

# introduction
## to the first edition

Delicious food is a celebration.

Over all the years I've been cooking I have never lost the thrill of serving, sharing and eating simple, delicious food.

To make all meals special is, for me, part of everyday life: crunchy toast with perfect avocado; a chicken sandwich made with real mayo and lots of fresh greens; a thick, glorious sabayon with biscotti to dip; spanking fresh cray tails; a beautifully poached egg; luscious passionfruit curd or a piece of aged sirloin — all inspire me to keep exploring and seeking out new and improved ways to prepare food.

Our access to fresh ingredients has never been so good, nor have the information networks about food and all the amazing and varied styles of serving, as well as flavours to combine and build with.

If you're stuck for what to cook or serve, the menus which follow the recipes (page 117) are combinations which I think work particularly well together. Many of the ideas in this book are versatile, I urge you to take time to seek ingredients rather than cook recipes. Think about the flavour of ingredients — some dishes need perfect and few ingredients, others need time and effort to build flavour and texture. Always look to enhance rather than bombard; use the best basic ingredients you can afford and enjoy the preparation as much as the eating.

Happy celebrating!

Kate Lamont, 2001.

# introduction
## to the second edition

In the six years since Celebrating was first published it seems the momentum around deliciousness, simplicity and seasonality has really found a place in the hearts and minds of everyone ... The reality is that every meal should be important, and a quick meal can also be a great meal. The accessibility of truly good quality fresh ingredients has never been better and wine to seems to be in everyone's fridge and enjoyed for all occasions, including a quiet evening at home. The thirst for knowledge about which wine to serve with what food has reached a new level. My enduring view is that wine and food are true companions and should be enjoyed together at every opportunity! And as our understanding grows we know that it is the way we treat ingredients, the way we build layers of flavour and develop an understanding of the weight and balance of flavours that creates the dining experiences we love so much.

Kate Lamont, 2007.

*canapés, finger food,*
*hors d'oeuvres, nibbles*

# seared scallop salsa

enough to top your favourite dish for 4

1 tablespoon extra virgin olive oil

1 tablespoon finely diced Spanish onion

4 tablespoons finely diced scallop meat

1 teaspoon salted baby capers

1 teaspoon chopped parsley

1 teaspoon chopped chives

2 tablespoons salmon caviar

zest and juice of 1 lime, zest finely chopped

pinch ground white pepper

You need to work quickly for this one.

Heat a medium sized frying pan until quite hot, add half the olive oil, all the onion and scallop meat and stir. Remove pan from the heat, fold in capers, herbs and salmon caviar, finish with the rest of the olive oil, lime juice and pepper.

Your scallop meat should be just under done, and all ingredients warmed through when serving.

*This salsa is so inviting and terrific on crunchy toast with a glass of champagne. A very versatile salsa, we often use it on simply grilled fish or pile it into baby cos and pass it around on platters.*

# salmon gravlax

makes 8 entrees or 30 canapés

180 g sea salt

250 g caster sugar

grated zest of 2 lemons and 2 oranges

1 cup chopped fennel fronds

¼ cup vodka

1 side of salmon boneless, skin on
— approximately 700 g

2 baguettes to serve

Mix salt, sugar, zest, fennel and vodka.

Place salmon on a large sheet of aluminium foil, skin side down. Gently rub the salt mixture into the fish. Pack excess on top. Wrap tightly in foil and keep in the refrigerator for 48 hours. Carefully remove from foil — a reasonable amount of liquid will come out of the fish. Blot the surface of the fish with kitchen towel to remove excess liquid. The salmon will keep refrigerated in cling wrap for 3 or 4 days after curing.

To serve: slice thinly on an angle across the fillet using a knife with a flexible blade. Pile on fresh bread with wedges of lime.

*Curing your own salmon with salt and sugar is simple to do and makes a delicious starter which can be dressed up or down to suit. Serve simply piled on fresh bread, or place in a single layer on plates topped with finely sliced fennel bulbs dressed with lemon, olive oil, pepper and salmon roe.*

# Tuna tartare

makes 8 entrees or 30 canapés

1 ripe, firm tomato

400 g fresh tuna

100 g wakame, or 20 g dry nori

¼ cup lemon juice

1 teaspoon sesame oil

½ teaspoon dried chilli flakes

2 tablespoons finely chopped red onion

2 tablespoons finely chopped chives

1 teaspoon minced ginger

1 tablespoon mayonnaise (recipe page 112)

salt and pepper, to season

30 crunchy toasts (recipe page 115)

Cut a cross in the skin at the base of the tomato, plunge in boiling water for 10 seconds to remove skin. Slice and remove seeds. Dice tuna and tomato finely. Chop wakame finely. If using nori, soak in water for 5 minutes to reconstitute, then chop finely. Mix seaweed with all other ingredients, except toasts, and season. Chill.

Serve on crunchy toasts.

*When I make this I use an imported frozen seaweed product, Chuuka Wakame.*
*It has a lovely vibrant colour and tastes of the sea, with a texture not found in the dried products.*
*Some fish markets sell wakame, but nori, available in supermarkets, still works well.*
*You can also serve tuna tartare as an entree, mounded onto plates with a dollop of crème fraîche and extra seaweed.*

# Eggplant jam

makes about 3 cups

4 medium eggplants

½ teaspoon salt, plus extra for salting

1½ cups olive oil

4 cloves garlic, minced

2 teaspoons sweet paprika

2 teaspoons cumin

1 teaspoon harissa

½ teaspoon pepper

¼ cup lemon juice

Cut stems from eggplants. Cut 2 cm strips from the eggplant skin, so that you get a striped eggplant. Discard the peel. Slice eggplant horizontally into 1 cm slices. Place into a colander and generously salt both sides of the slices. Stand for 30 minutes. Rinse salt off each slice and pat dry. Pre-heat oven to 190°C. Using olive oil, brush both sides of eggplant and place in a single layer on an oven tray. Bake until cooked through, about 30 minutes. Meanwhile, in a food processor combine garlic, paprika, cumin, harissa, salt, pepper and lemon juice to form a paste. Once the eggplant has cooked, and is still warm, process with the paste until blended. Add extra salt and pepper to taste.

Serve with warm flatbread (recipe page 114).

*This jam, first introduced to Lamonts by Joanne Weir, is a firm customer favourite.*

# Prawn and paprika pancakes

makes 18

1 cup finely sliced spring onions

2 tablespoons olive oil

200 g green prawn flesh

¾ cup plain flour

½ cup chickpea flour

½ teaspoon baking powder

salt and pepper, to season

2 teaspoons paprika

1–1¼ cups cold water

vegetable oil, to fry

chives and crème fraîche, to serve

Fry spring onions in 2 tablespoons of olive oil until soft, but not coloured. Cool. Slice prawn flesh finely and combine with all ingredients to make a batter the consistency of heavy cream. Set aside to rest for 2 hours. Shallow fry spoonfuls of batter in hot oil to form pancakes about 5 cm in diameter. Drain on paper towel to remove excess oil.

Serve hot with a little crème fraîche and chopped chives.

*Another Joanne Weir inspired idea, these are fantastic eaten hot straight from the grill. Seek out some smokey paprika — it will make a big difference to the final taste. You can substitute scallops or mussels for the prawns, and if you make them very thin they can be sandwiched together with crème fraîche.*

# Mushroom risotto bites

makes 40

### Risotto:

50 g dried porcini mushrooms

2 cups hot water

1 brown onion

1 clove garlic

salt and pepper, to season

500 g arborio rice

¾ cup olive oil

1 cup white wine

5 cups chicken stock (recipe page 108)

¾ cup parmesan, grated

### Crumb:

2 cups breadcrumbs

½ cup parmesan, grated

1 egg

1 cup milk

1 cup plain flour

oil, to fry

Soak mushrooms in hot water for 1 hour. Drain and reserve liquid. Dice onion finely, mince garlic, mix and sauté over medium heat in olive oil until translucent. Finely slice mushrooms, add to onion and cook for 3 or 4 minutes. Season with salt and pepper. Add rice and stir to coat each grain with oil. Cook rice for 1 minute then turn heat to high. Add white wine and stir vigorously until it is absorbed, then add the mushroom liquid and stir until it is absorbed. Reduce heat to medium. Meanwhile, heat stock until just simmering. Gradually add stock, a ladleful at a time. Stir as you go and continue to add stock as the rice absorbs the liquid. You will end up with a creamy mixture that has individual grains of rice. Add more salt and pepper if required. Fold in parmesan.

Make bites: tip risotto onto a tray and cool. Form into balls about the size of walnuts. Mix breadcrumbs with parmesan. Whisk milk and egg together. Roll bites in flour, then egg wash then parmesan crumb. Deep fry until golden, about 4–5 minutes.

Serve hot with rocket pesto (recipe page 113).

*This risotto also makes a tasty entree. I usually drizzle each portion with piquant olive oil before serving.*

# Hommus

makes about 3 cups

550 g dried chickpeas
2 tablespoons tahini
1 garlic clove, crushed
2 tablespoons lemon juice
1½ teaspoons ground cumin
1½ teaspoons salt
½ teaspoon pepper
⅔ cup olive oil

Soak chickpeas overnight in a litre of water. Drain and cook in fresh water until soft, about 45 minutes, and keep warm — if they're at all firm they won't puree. In a food processor, process warm chickpeas, tahini, garlic, lemon juice, cumin, salt and pepper until finely chopped. Slowly drizzle in olive oil, and process to a thick, smooth paste.

Serve with crunchy toasts or basil toasts (recipes page 115).

# Avocado crostini

makes 24 toasts

2 perfectly ripe avocados

salt and pepper, to season

2 tablespoons lemon juice

24 crunchy toasts (recipe page 115)

Peel and roughly dice the avocados. Season and add lemon juice. With a fork, gently mash the avocado to a coarse consistency.

Serve piled onto crunchy toasts.

# Grilled parmesan polenta

makes 36 bite-size serves

2 cups milk

3 cups chicken stock

300 g fine polenta

salt and pepper, to season

¾ cup grated parmesan

75 g butter

2 tablespoons olive oil

1 cup basil leaves, sliced finely

Combine milk and stock in a large pot. Bring to boil, remove from heat and slowly whisk in polenta. Return to stove and cook over a low heat for about 30 minutes, stirring with a wooden spoon. Be careful that the mixture doesn't catch on the bottom of the pot. Season and add cheese, butter and olive oil. Line a tray (approximately 25 cm x 15 cm x 2 cm) with baking paper. Pour polenta into tray and smooth top with a wet spatula. Cool. When firm, turn out and cut into bite-size squares. Top with a little extra parmesan and the basil. Grill until cheese is melted and serve warm.

*Grilled parmesan polenta can also be served as an accompaniment to a main course, such as marinated beef (recipe page 52). To serve, cut cooled, firm polenta into eight pieces, drizzle with olive oil and grill on a barbecue to reheat and crisp edges, about 5 minutes.*

# greens, salads, vegetables

# Ricotta gnocchi with pancetta and cabernet vinegar

serves 6

### Gnocchi:

500 g ricotta, drained overnight

3 eggs

¼ cup grated parmesan

¾ cup flour

salt

olive oil for tossing

### Vinegar:

200 g streaky smoked pancetta

100 g salted butter

2 tablespoons red wine vinegar

salt and pepper

parmesan and flat-leaf parsley to serve

Hang the ricotta overnight to firm. Crack eggs into a bowl and gently break up with a fork, add ricotta and gently fold in parmesan. Incorporate the ricotta mixture with the flour to a smooth dough. Divide dough into 4. Roll each piece into a sausage shape on a well floured bench and with a sharp knife cut into 2 cm squares. Blanche in simmering salted water for 6 minutes, drain and toss in a little olive oil. These gnocchi can be served immediately or warmed when used later. Crisp pancetta. Melt butter in pan, add vinegar, salt and pepper.

Serve sauce with warm gnocchi, pancetta and grated parmesan and parsley.

*Be sure to hang the ricotta overnight, this will ensure that the gnocchi are as light as air, and be bold with the vinegar — it gives a fabulous tang.*

# Tomatoes with basil and cream

serves 8

16 small ripe tomatoes

2 tablespoons white vinegar

1 cup cream

salt and pepper, to season

1 cup basil leaves

Cut a cross in the skin at the base of each tomato, plunge in boiling water for 10 seconds to remove skin. Core and chill. Combine vinegar and cream, and season. Finely slice basil and add to cream mixture. Place tomatoes in a shallow dish, cover with cream and basil mixture. Leave for a couple of hours, if possible, as the flavours improve.

*I first ate these tomatoes at my grandmother's.*
*I didn't believe her at first when she gave me the recipe — they taste so good and the recipe is so simple!*
*They look particularly inviting if you platter them and present them to the table.*

# Asparagus and wild rice salad

serves 8

3 cups wild rice

2 cups long grain white rice

500 g asparagus

120 g chives (2 bunches)

500 g cherry tomatoes

¼ cup sherry vinegar

⅔ cup olive oil

1 cup caramelised onion (recipe page 110)

salt and pepper, to season

Boil each type of rice separately in a generous amount of salted water until tender, but still holding its shape. Rinse under cold water. Drain well. Trim ends from asparagus and blanch in a pot of boiling water for 1–2 minutes. Refresh asparagus immediately by plunging in cold water. Cut into 4 cm lengths. Snip chives into 2 cm pieces. Cut cherry tomatoes in half. Mix vinegar, oil and seasoning to make dressing. Gently toss rice, asparagus, tomatoes, chives and caramelised onion with dressing and season.

*I love the sherry vinegar in this salad as it seems to enhance the nutty flavour of the wild rice. If you can't find sherry vinegar you could substitute red wine vinegar.*

# Caramelised pumpkin and shallots

serves 8

1½ kg pumpkin

4 tablespoons olive oil

salt and pepper, to season

24 shallots

10 stalks fresh thyme

2 tablespoons red wine vinegar

Preheat oven to 180°C. Cut pumpkin into 16 wedges. Drizzle with olive oil, season and brown on grill plate, or barbecue if available. Transfer to an oven tray. Meanwhile, peel shallots. Sauté in a pan with thyme and olive oil until golden. Add shallots to pumpkin and bake until soft, about 30 minutes. Splash pumpkin and shallots with red wine vinegar while hot and serve.

*Occasionally you can buy gorgeous little green and white striped pumpkins — in the markets near my home they're called Japanese pumpkins — with a real sweetness of flavour.*
*Having said that though, new season Queensland Blues are still a personal favourite.*

# Field mushroom and rocket salad

serves 8

8 slices sourdough bread, about 1 cm thick

olive oil, to cook

salt and pepper, to season

16 medium field mushrooms

10 stalks fresh thyme

4 medium tomatoes

8 cups small rocket leaves

½ cup aioli (recipe page 112)

shaved parmesan, to serve

Preheat oven to 180ºC. To make croutons, cut the bread into 1 cm cubes, drizzle with olive oil, season with salt and pepper and bake until golden, about 10 minutes. Wipe mushrooms free of any grit. Slice stalks off at base and discard. Place the mushrooms on a baking tray, cap side down, drizzle with olive oil, season and scatter with thyme. Roast for about 7 minutes or until cooked through, but make sure they're still juicy. Cut a cross in the skin at the base of each tomato, plunge in boiling water for 10 seconds to remove skin. Core, deseed and chill. Slice tomatoes into long slivers and mix with croutons and rocket. Toss with a little aioli.

To serve: put 2 warm mushrooms on each plate, cover with rocket, drizzle with remaining aioli and top with parmesan.

*This simple salad is great as a starter, or as a main after a bowl of soup. It can be made more substantial by adding some sautéed asparagus and substituting fresh goats cheese for the parmesan.*

# Pasta with olives and herbs

serves 8

4 medium tomatoes

2 anchovies

1 tablespoon capers

2 cloves garlic

⅓ cup of mixed fresh herbs
(basil, oregano, thyme, parsley, marjoram)

½ cup Ligurian olives

½ cup green olives, pitted

6 tablespoons fruity extra virgin olive oil

1 tablespoon red wine vinegar

500 g shaped pasta

Cut a cross in the skin at the base of each tomato, plunge in boiling water for 10 seconds to remove skin. Deseed and dice tomatoes. Cut anchovies into slivers. Chop capers roughly. Chop garlic finely. Chop herbs roughly in a large bowl. Add tomatoes, anchovies, olives, capers, garlic, oil and vinegar. Mix well and set aside to rest for 1 hour. Cook pasta until al dente then add to herb mixture. Toss quickly and serve immediately.

*This pasta dish is a real celebration of fresh tastes and is best served at virtually room temperature —*
*it seems to me that that's when the flavours are at their zenith.*
*I like to use perfectly ripe tomatoes, and pasta shapes such as strozzapreti or orecchiette.*
*The little pieces of olive and caper sit snugly inside the pasta giving powerful flavour bites.*

# Potato, asparagus and pea salad

serves 8

750 g gourmet potatoes

¾ cup olive oil, plus 2 tablespoons

500 g fresh peas in pods

500 g asparagus

salt and pepper to season

150 g snow peas

⅓ cup fresh chervil

2 cups baby English spinach

2 quartered rinds preserved lemon
(or 2 tablespoons fresh lemon zest)

¼ cup lemon juice

Boil potatoes whole in salted water until tender, about 15 minutes. When cool enough to handle, but still warm, cut into quarters. Season and toss in ¼ cup of oil. Shell peas and cook in simmering salted water for about 5 minutes. Refresh in cold water, drain and add to potatoes. Trim ends from asparagus and cut into thirds. Sauté in the 2 tablespoons of olive oil with seasoning for about 3 minutes. Add to potatoes. Slice uncooked snow peas into thin strips and pick chervil leaves from stems. Add snow peas, chervil and spinach to potatoes. Finely chop preserved lemon rinds and mix into salad. Make dressing by combining lemon juice and remaining oil. Gently toss salad with dressing.

*This is one of my springtime favourites. I try to buy foxton or desiree potatoes, as they stay firm and have a good texture for salad. Lemon really brings out the flavour of peas.*
*When using preserved lemon, discard the flesh and slice the rinds as thinly as you can.*

# Greek salad with Yarra Valley Persian fetta

serves 8

250 g tin Yarra Valley Persian Fetta

8 ripe tomatoes

4 Lebanese cucumbers

2 red onions

¼ cup red wine vinegar

1 cup black olives
(ideally Ligurian or Niçoise)

1 cup flat-leaf parsley, plucked from stalks

150 g of baby English spinach

salt and pepper, to taste

Drain fetta and reserve oil from tin. Remove cores and cut tomatoes into wedges. Trim ends from cucumbers and slice. Finely slice onions into rings. Mix the reserved oil and vinegar to make dressing. Gently toss all ingredients together.

The flavours of this salad intensify if made a couple of hours before serving.

*Yarra Valley Dairy in Victoria produce a wonderful cheese they call Persian fetta. It comes in small tins and has a marvellous flavour, but you could substitute it with other, or your own, marinated fetta.*

# snap pea salad with pan juices

serves 8

1 cup pan juices

500 g snap peas

500 g snow peas

2 cups snow pea shoots

½ cup fresh mint leaves

salt and pepper, to season

This salad is to accompany roasted meat. Reserve 1 cup of pan juices from roasting tray. Top and tail the peas and trim the base from the shoots. Blanch peas in boiling water and refresh by plunging in cold water. Drain. Cut mint into thin strips. Mix the peas and shoots together. Season. Warm the pan juices and mix with the mint. Pour over the peas and serve.

# Rocket salad

serves 8

200 g rocket

1 tablespoon red wine vinegar

3 tablespoons olive oil

salt and pepper, to season

75 g parmesan cheese

Pick through rocket to ensure perfect leaves. Combine vinegar, oil, salt and pepper to make dressing. Shave parmesan. Toss all ingredients together and serve.

# Wilted cucumber salad

serves 8s

3 cucumbers

1 tablespoon salt

1 finely chopped red onion

½ cup sour cream

pepper, to season

Peel cucumbers then deseed by slicing in half lengthwise and scooping out seeds. Slice as thinly as possible, mix with salt and leave in a colander for 30 minutes. Wash thoroughly in cold water and squeeze tightly to remove as much liquid as possible. The cucumber should be almost transparent. Finely chop the onion and mix with sour cream. Season well with pepper, mix with cucumber and serve.

*Snap pea salad with pan juices is photographed with Pumpkin and proscuitto stuffed turkey on page 60.*
*Rocket salad, photographed with My favourite marinated beef on page 52.*
*Wilted cucumber salad, photographed with Lamb koftas on page 54.*

meat, fish,
poultry, seafood

# Braised lamb with endamame salad

serves 6

6 lamb rumps

salt and pepper

olive oil to cook

2 carrots

4 sticks celery

2 onions

1 bulb garlic

2 cups red wine

2 litres beef stock

*For the salad:*

300 g chick peas

4 tablespoons olive oil

salt and pepper

300 g broad beans, shelled if fresh

500 g endamame

2 tablespoons chopped dill

2 tablespoons picked chervil

*For the mayonnaise*: use the basic mayonnaise recipe on page 112 and add 1 teaspoon smoky paprika to the egg yolk

Season the lamb with salt and pepper and seal until well browned in a little olive oil, remove. Ideally you could do this in the braising pan you will use to cook the lamb, which will ensure all the flavours will be captured in the final meal. Chop vegetables coarsely and add to pan. Deglaze the pan with the red wine and reduce by about half, add the stock and lamb, cover pan and cook in a 160°C oven for 2 hours or until the lamb is very tender and almost falling apart. Take lamb from pan and strain cooking juices, discard vegetables and reduce sauce down to about one cup. When serving lamb, coat with this reduced sauce and reheat if necessary.

Soak chick peas overnight in water then simmer until soft, drain and douse in the olive oil and season with salt and pepper and reserve. Meanwhile simmer the broad beans until tender, refresh in cold water and then peel to remove the outer casing. Pop the endamame out of their pods. Mix the endamame and broad beans with the warm chick peas and the herbs.

*By braising the lamb you create deliciously tender meat and a beautiful tasty sauce to coat. The combination of the endamame and the broad beans gives a great 'savoury' feel to the salad — these flavours have a wonderful autumn sense to them and the powerfully tasty mayonnaise offers a silky touch.*

# My favourite marinated beef

serves 8

12 cloves garlic

2 cups soy sauce

1 cup cider vinegar

⅓ cup balsamic vinegar

1 red chilli

1 tablespoon brown sugar

2½–3 kg piece of Scotch fillet or tenderloin

Mince garlic to a paste. Mix soy sauce and vinegars. Chop chilli finely. Mix garlic with chilli and sugar and rub into beef. Marinate beef in soy sauce and vinegar mix for at least 24 hours. Barbecue beef as a whole piece to your liking.

Serve sliced on grilled polenta (recipe page 26) with rocket salad (recipe page 46).

*I like to use Scotch fillet and barbecue the piece whole; the outside gets very charry and the inside stays succulent. A 2 kg piece of beef will take about 40 minutes to cook medium-rare on a barbecue. Seal the meat on a high heat and then adjust to a medium flame. Let the meat rest for 30 minutes after it's cooked to retain its juiciness.*

# Lamb koftas

makes 16 sticks

½ cup pine nuts

16 bamboo satay sticks

2 onions

2 cloves garlic

olive oil, to cook

salt and pepper, to season

½ cup fresh mint leaves

1 kg lamb mince

1 tablespoon chickpea (or plain) flour

2 teaspoons cinnamon

2 teaspoons cardamom

Preheat oven to 175ºC. Toast pine nuts until golden, about 10 minutes, and chop roughly. Soak sticks in water for 30 minutes. Chop onions and garlic finely and sauté in a little olive oil until soft. Season. Finely chop mint leaves. Mix all ingredients together. Shape a handful of lamb mince around each stick and chill. Barbecue for 10–15 minutes, turning regularly until well browned on the outside and just pink on the inside.

*These are great picnic and snack food, as they're just as good cold and transport well.*

# Crispy roasted spatchcock

serves 8

1 tablespoon sea salt

1 teaspoon whole Szechuan peppercorns

1 teaspoon whole black peppercorns

4 juniper berries

8 spatchcocks, partially boned and flattened

4 tablespoons olive oil

1 tablespoon chopped fresh sage

8 field mushrooms

8 cups mixed salad greens

16 roasted tomatoes (recipe page 111)

*Honey mustard dressing:*

2 egg yolks

1 tablespoon grain mustard

1 tablespoon honey

4 tablespoons lime juice

1/3 cup sherry vinegar

1¼ cups olive oil

salt and pepper, to season

In a frying pan, warm salt and peppercorns over a moderate heat until aromatic, about 5 minutes. Cool and grind together with juniper berries. Marinate spatchcocks in oil, sage and pepper mix for up to 24 hours. Preheat oven to 180°C. Trim mushrooms and drizzle with spatchcock marinade. Roast mushrooms for 10 minutes. Keep warm. Roast spatchcocks for 25–30 minutes, until golden and crisp.

To make dressing: mix yolks with mustard, honey, lime juice and vinegar in a food processor. With the motor running, drizzle oil in slowly. Season. Lightly dress the salad greens with half the dressing.

To serve: layer tomatoes, mushrooms and salad greens on plates. Place spatchcocks on top and drizzle with remaining dressing.

*It's worth taking the time to remove the ribcage from the spatchcocks (instructions page 106, follow up to point 7). Partly boned birds cook quickly, leaving the meat succulent. The marinade is aromatic and presents a crisp finish, making a good contrast to the dressing. To create a sturdier, thicker dressing, whisk by hand.*

# Mediterranean-flavours stuffed turkey

4 red capsicums

½ cup olive oil, plus 2 tablespoons

2 medium eggplants

½ cup fresh mint leaves

½ cup flat-leaf parsley

250 g fresh breadcrumbs

120 g pitted kalamata olives

½ cup crème fraîche

350 g fetta

1 boned turkey (instructions page 106)

salt and pepper, to season

Preheat oven to 180°C. Slice tops from capsicums, leave whole and remove seeds. Place cut side down on a baking tray and brush with 2 tablespoons of oil. Roast for about 35 minutes, or until skins begin to colour and blister. Cool, remove skins and slice down to lay flat. Dice eggplants, salt and wash if desired, and sauté in ½ cup of olive oil until soft. Chop mint and parsley and mix with all the stuffing ingredients except capsicum. Season. Lay the boned turkey out flat and season. Cover with pieces of capsicum. Form the stuffing into a log and place down the centre of the bird on top of the capsicum. Roll the turkey up and tie securely.

Roast and serve hot or cold.

*Not just for Christmas, turkey is an often forgotten meat, available and delicious year round.*
*This stuffing is also great with chicken, but you'll need to reduce the quantities.*
*A boned turkey takes about half to two-thirds the cooking time of a whole turkey — a 6 kg boned turkey, for example, will take a little over 1½ hours in a moderate oven.*

# Pumpkin and prosciutto stuffed turkey

500 g sturdy bread

1 kg pumpkin

salt and pepper, to season

olive oil, to drizzle

200 g prosciutto

2 celery stalks

6 shallots

3 cloves garlic

½ cup chopped fresh oregano and parsley

100 g dried figs

50 g butter

¼ cup chicken stock (recipe page 109)

1 turkey, boned or whole

Preheat oven to 190°C. Cut bread into 1 cm cubes, season and bake for about 10 minutes. Skin pumpkin and cut into 2 cm cubes. Season and drizzle with olive oil, then bake for about 20 minutes. Slice celery into 1 cm pieces. Dice shallots finely. Mince garlic. Sauté celery, garlic and shallots in the remaining oil. Chop figs into quarters. Slice prosciutto into 1 cm strips. Gently mix all ingredients together and stuff turkey. Roast and serve hot.

*I love the vibrancy and crispness of Snap pea salad (recipe page 46) to accompany roast turkey.*
*The pan juices begin to wilt the snow pea shoots, and the peas retain their crunch.*

# Hiramasa carpaccio

serves 8

50 g chopped coriander
zest of 1 lime
40 g salt
20 g sugar
600 g hiramasa
1 tablespoon lime juice
zest of two limes
4 tablespoons olive oil
1 cup assorted baby leaves
salt and pepper

Combine coriander, lime zest, salt and sugar, rub into the hiramasa and marinate for 6 to 8 hours.

To serve: slice fish thinly across the grain and arrange in centre of the plate. To make a dressing mix lime juice and olive oil. Scatter with baby leaves and zest. Season with salt and pepper and drizzle with dressing.

*This fish is so velvety you can feel it doing you good! I love it simply scattered with baby greens and lime but on occasion I have used caramelised onion and snipped young asparagus to give a more substantial finish, or you may like to add pickled cucumber and ginger.*

# Crab pasta

serves 8

1 cup white wine

1 cup fish stock (recipe page 109)

zest of 3 lemons

salt and pepper, to season

1 cup fresh coriander leaves

750 g fresh crab meat

500 g linguini

good quality olive oil, to serve

Reduce white wine by half in a flat pan on the stove over high heat. Add stock and reduce again by half. Add lemon zest, seasoning and half the coriander. Add crab meat and cook for about 2 minutes. Meanwhile, cook and drain linguini. Coat pasta with oil while still warm, then add to crab and heat through. Add remaining coriander.

Serve immediately, drizzled with the best olive oil you can find.

*This is a really delicate and elegant pasta dish,*
*a great example of letting simple fresh flavours speak for themselves.*

# Crayfish tails

serves 8

8 cloves garlic

1 teaspoon salt

2 teaspoons black peppercorns

150 g fresh coriander

2 tablespoons lime juice

8 green crayfish tails, shells on

limes, to serve

Crush garlic with salt to form a paste. Crush peppercorns to resemble cracked black pepper. Wash coriander plants well, strip roots of loose fibres. Pluck leaves from coriander and reserve. Chop stalks and roots finely. Add lime juice and mix with pepper and garlic paste. Leaving the shells on, use a large knife to slice through the belly of the crayfish, creating a butterfly effect. Mix crayfish with seasonings and leave for an hour. Barbecue until the meat is opaque, about 7 minutes. Serve immediately scattered with coriander leaves and lime halves.

*Eating crayfish cooked this way is such a treat.*
*The tails stay moist and the lime juice cuts through the richness of the meat.*

# Whole baked salmon with lentil sauce

serves 8

1 salmon — 2½–3 kg

1 lemon

salt and pepper, to season

4 tablespoons olive oil

*Sauce:*

4 whole cardamom pods

2 tablespoons olive oil

½ cup Puy lentils

3 cups chicken stock (recipe page 108)

3 tablespoons fish sauce

1 teaspoon of turmeric

1½ cups cream

salt and pepper, to season

2 spring onions

juice of 2 limes

Preheat oven to 180°C. Ensure that the salmon is gutted and scaled. Cut lemon into slices and place inside salmon. Season salmon inside and out. Rub olive oil over the skin. Wrap in foil, place on a tray and bake for 35 to 40 minutes, until just cooked.

To make the sauce: flavour oil with cardamom by heating the pods and oil in a frying pan over high heat. Discard pods. Add lentils to oil with stock, turmeric and fish sauce. Bring to the boil and reduce by half. Add cream and seasoning (easy on the salt, as the fish sauce is salty) and simmer until the sauce is thick and the lentils are tender. Slice the spring onions finely. Stir the lime juice and half the spring onions into the sauce. Carefully remove salmon from foil and place on a warmed platter. Pour sauce over the whole fish, scatter with remaining spring onions and serve.

*Serve this fish with lots of crusty bread to mop up the sauce. Be sure to be generous with the lime juice, and add it right at the end — it gives the sauce a fabulous pungency.*

# scallop and smoked salmon lasagne

serves 8

5 fresh lasagne sheets, approximately 20 cm x 15 cm

oil, to brush

500 g fresh salmon

salt and pepper, to season

100 g salmon roe

30 scallops

4 cups large leafed English spinach

250 g crème fraîche

16 slices smoked salmon

3 tablespoons fresh dill, to serve

fruity olive oil, to serve

Cook lasagne sheets individually in a large pot of boiling water for about 3 minutes. Refresh by plunging into cold water, blot dry and brush with oil. Poach fresh salmon for about 5 minutes, leaving slightly undercooked, season and, once cooled, flake and mix with roe. Cook scallops in a frying pan, season, cool and cut in half horizontally. Blanch spinach, refresh in cold water, gently squeeze to remove excess and pat dry. Lightly brush a 26 cm springform tin with oil. Lay cling wrap in a cross in tin with plenty of extra at each end. Brush wrap with oil. Cut lasagne sheets to fit neatly into the tin, spread one side of each sheet with crème fraîche and season. To assemble, layer ingredients as follows: lasagne sheet, crème fraîche up; half the smoked salmon; half the spinach; half the scallops; lasagne sheet, crème fraîche side down; half the fresh salmon; lasagne sheet, crème fraîche side down; remaining smoked salmon, then spinach, then scallops; lasagne sheet, crème fraîche side down; remaining fresh salmon; final lasagne sheet, crème fraîche side down. Cover tightly with the cling wrap and chill for 6 hours. To turn out, open the cling wrap and remove the sides of the tin. Invert on a serving platter.

To serve: slice into portions and drizzle with fruity olive oil and finely chopped dill.

*'Lasagne' is a bit of a misnomer for this dish, as it's served cold, and there isn't a tomato in sight. It takes a bit of preparation to make, but it's a beautiful entree and well worth the effort.*

# Yabbie salad

serves 8

40 yabbies

1 fennel bulb

1 red onion

½ cup salsa verde (recipe page 111)

300 g baby cos leaves

salt and pepper, to season

Cook yabbies in boiling salted water for between 5 and 8 minutes, or until they float. It is important that the pot is large enough to stay boiling as you put the yabbies in. Cool, peel and remove entrails. Reserve meat from claws. Trim and slice fennel and onion finely and mix with the claw meat and a little salsa verde. Portion cos leaves onto plates, adding onion and fennel mix. Slice yabbies in half lengthways and place on cos leaves. Drizzle with remaining salsa verde, season and serve.

*If possible, purchase the yabbies live and put them in the freezer for 30 minutes before cooking. The claw meat is particularly sweet so be sure to extract the meat and include it in the salad.*

# Snapper with Indian spiced potatoes

serves 8

*Indian spices*:

3 tablespoons cumin seeds

1 teaspoon fennel seeds

1½ tablespoons red mustard seeds

1 teaspoon chilli flakes

3 tablespoons sesame seeds

1 teaspoon turmeric

1 teaspoon black peppercorns

1 teaspoon sea salt

1 cup olive oil, plus extra for cooking

8 medium potatoes

4 red onions

8 fillets of snapper (about 180 g each)

salt and pepper, to season

400 g stringless green beans

½ cup natural yoghurt

In a dry frying pan cook the spices over a moderate heat until fragrant, 3–5 minutes. Cool and grind. Mix with 1 cup of olive oil. Parboil the potatoes until they are barely cooked. Cool and slice. Peel and slice the onions thinly, toss in 2 tablespoons of the oil and spice mix and fry until softened. Keep warm. Brush potatoes with the oil and spice mix and pan fry until golden. Meanwhile, pan fry or grill the fish, seasoned with salt and pepper, about 10 minutes. Trim the beans and cook in simmering salted water. Mix yoghurt with 2 tablespoons of the oil and spice mix.

To serve: place slices of warm potato on serving plates, pile the beans and fish on top of potatoes, scatter with onions and drizzle with the yoghurt.

*desserts, puddings,*
*cakes, biscuits*

# Pavlova roll with passionfruit cream

serves 8

4 egg whites

1 cup caster sugar

1 teaspoon vinegar (I use brown)

1 teaspoon vanilla

2 level dessertspoons cornflour

*Passionfruit cream:*

pulp of 4 passionfruit

1½ cups whipped cream

(fold together and leave aside)

Beat egg whites until stiff, add sugar gradually and beat until sugar is completely dissolved. Add vinegar and vanilla, then fold in cornflour. Line a lamington tin with greaseproof paper and sprinkle lightly with caster sugar and a little cornflour, then pour the mixture on and smooth out. Bake at 150°C until firm to touch — about 15 mins. On a bench lay down a tea towel with another sheet of greaseproof paper on top of it. Sprinkle more caster sugar and immediately flip pavlova onto it. Carefully remove the lining paper. When cool, trim edges to neaten and spread with ⅔ of the whipped cream and passionfruit. Using the tea towel, roll it up.

If the top cracks just decorate with remaining cream. Serve any remaining cream with slices of roll.

*So simple and so good!!*

# summer pudding

makes 8

400 g raspberries

400 g blueberries

400 g strawberries

1 cup water

1 cup sugar

24 slices day old white bread

8 stackable teacups

thickened cream and extra berries, to serve

Place berries, water and sugar in a saucepan. Bring to boil then remove from heat and cool. Drain berries and reserve syrup. Remove crusts from bread and cut to line cups — rounds for lids and bases, and strips for the sides. Dip each piece of bread in syrup then gently line the cups. Fill each lined cup with berries and a small amount of syrup. Put a well dipped 'lid' on top. Stack cups 2 high and refrigerate overnight or for up to 3 days. Each pudding needs to be weighed down to compress it. Either switch the cups over after 12 hours, or add a third empty cup to the top of each stack. To remove from cups, run a knife around each pudding to loosen, then turn out.

Serve with remaining syrup, extra berries and cream.

*Summer pudding is a real favourite with my family, and my customers. Making them as individual servings is easy if you use stackable cups which weight the puddings so they hold together and soak up all the berry juices.*

# Grilled figs and chilled sabayon

serves 8

*Figs:*

½ cup caster sugar

½ cup water

24 small purple figs

2 tablespoons soft brown sugar

*Sabayon:*

8 egg yolks

½ cup caster sugar

1 cup sweet white wine

(or ½ cup brandy and ½ cup water)

1 cup cream

To grill the figs: mix caster sugar and water together and simmer until sugar dissolves. Cool. Trim tops from figs and squash them gently so they open a little at the top. Place on a baking tray. Preheat grill to medium. Put a teaspoon of sugar syrup into the top of each fig and sprinkle with brown sugar. Place under grill (or in a moderate oven) and cook until the tops caramelise and figs are warmed through, about 3 minutes.

To make the sabayon: put yolks, sugar and wine in a bowl over a pot of simmering water and whisk until very thick, about 10 to 15 minutes. Be careful not to overheat. Remove from heat and cool. Whisk cream to soft peaks and fold into the sabayon.

*Sabayon is so beautiful and smooth and rich. It's fantastic slathered on poached or grilled fruit, great to dip biscotti in and has even been known to be eaten straight from the bowl!*

# Chocolate tart

makes a 26 cm tart — enough for 8

*Pastry:*

125 g cold unsalted butter

1½ cups plain flour

pinch of salt

2 tablespoons icing sugar

1 egg

*Filling:*

500 g dark chocolate

250 g unsalted butter

3 tablespoons icing sugar

3 whole eggs

5 egg yolks

thickened cream and Dutch cocoa, to serve

Cut cold butter into 1 cm cubes. In a food processor combine butter with dry ingredients. Add egg and process until the mixture forms a dough. Remove dough from processor, form into a ball, wrap in cling wrap and refrigerate for 30 minutes. Roll dough on a floured bench to ½ cm thick. Line a 26 cm tart tin with the pastry. Refrigerate for 1 hour. Preheat oven to 180ºC. Blind bake pastry for 15 minutes by covering the base with greaseproof paper and filling the tart with rice, dried beans or pastry weights. Remove weights and paper and bake pastry for a further 5 minutes to dry the base.

To make the filling: melt chocolate and butter together in a bowl over a pot of simmering water. In a separate bowl, whisk icing sugar, eggs and yolks until thick. Gently fold melted chocolate into egg mixture. Spoon into pastry case and cook at 170ºC for 15 minutes until barely set. If desired, dust tart with cocoa. Serve with cream.

*Use the very best dark chocolate you can find for this dense tart.*
*As a variation you can spread praline (recipe page 110) in the cooked case and tip the filling over it, then bake.*

# Liqueur fruits semi-freddo

serves 8

*Liqueur fruits:*

200 g dried figs

200 g almonds

4 tablespoons cherries (fresh if available)

200 g raisins

4 tablespoons port

*Semi-freddo:*

8 large eggs, separated

2 vanilla pods, seeds scraped out

4 cups cream

120 g caster sugar

pinch of salt

To make liqueur fruits: preheat oven to 180°C. Roast almonds until aromatic and toasted, about 5 minutes. Chop figs and almonds. Mix with cherries, raisins and port. Soak for 24 hours.

To make semi-freddo: beat egg yolks with vanilla seeds and sugar for about 10 minutes to form a thick pale mixture. Whisk cream to a similar consistency. Whisk egg whites with a pinch of salt to firm peaks. Fold all 3 mixtures together with the liqueur fruits. Pour into a container, cover with cling wrap and freeze for at least 6 hours. Keeps for about 3 days.

*A semi-freddo is a bit like delicious air. It is disarmingly light and irresistible even after a big meal. Semi-freddo freezes quite hard, so leave it out of the freezer for about 15 minutes before serving.*

# White chocolate mousse

serves 8

200 g best quality white chocolate

4 eggs, separated

100 g unsalted butter, softened

2 teaspoons caster sugar

Chop chocolate and melt gently in a large bowl over a pot of simmering water. Remove bowl from heat and beat in egg yolks, one at a time. Add butter, beating well until mixture is glossy and smooth. Whip egg whites until soft peaks form. Sprinkle sugar over egg whites and continue to whip until satiny. Fold quickly and thoroughly into chocolate mixture. Transfer mixture to a serving bowl or individual bowls and chill for at least 4 hours. Allow mousse to come to room temperature before serving. If in a large bowl, a tablespoon dipped into boiling water will enable you to spoon out perfectly shaped quenelles of mousse.

Serve with poached or fresh fruit.

*This is very creamy and chocolatey, and you really do need the best white chocolate you can find — I like to use Valrhona or Callebaut. It's important not to overheat the chocolate as you melt it — I usually turn the heat right down, or even off. Be sure to leave the mousse out of the fridge for an hour or so before serving.*

# Poached strawberries

serves 8

1 kg fresh strawberries

1 cup sugar

2 cups water

Wash and hull strawberries. Simmer sugar and water together until reduced by half. Add strawberries and bring back to boil. Remove from heat and allow strawberries to cool in the syrup. Serve with cream, ice-cream or white chocolate mousse.

*Poaching strawberries turns imperfect fruit into fragrant, soft morsels. They are most delicious with ripe berries, but firm and slightly under-ripe berries will be really enhanced by this recipe.*
*Serve just warm with vanilla ice-cream and praline (recipe page 110).*

# Plum and polenta cake

makes a 26 cm cake — enough for 8

*Cake:*

7 plums

250 g sugar

2 teaspooons vanilla essence

5 eggs

1 cup white wine

1 cup vegetable oil, or mild flavoured olive oil

310 g plain flour

120 g polenta

1 teaspoon baking powder

1 teaspoon cinnamon

*Syrup:*

175 g sugar

⅓ cup water

½ cup orange juice

Preheat oven to 180°C. Cut plums in half and arrange cut side down in a greased, papered 26 cm cake tin. In an electric mixer, whisk sugar, vanilla essence and eggs until foamy. Add white wine and oil slowly, mixing at a gentler speed. In a separate bowl, sift dry ingredients together. Fold dry and wet ingredients together. Pour over plums. Bake for 1 hour. Meanwhile, boil syrup ingredients together. Remove cake from oven. Leave in tin and immediately prick cake 10 times with a skewer. Pour syrup over cake and cool in the tin.

*I love this cake! Texturally it is both moist and crumbly, and the sweetness of the fruit really enhances the almost savoury flavours of the cake.*
*When in season, you can make this recipe using nectarines, peaches or pears.*

# Mango ice-cream and lime syrup

makes 20 generous scoops

*Ice-cream:*

1 cup caster sugar

²/₃ cup water

3 egg yolks

juice of 1 lime

2 cups soft whipped cream

1½ cups pureed mango
(about 4 fresh mangoes)

*Lime syrup:*

2 cups white sugar

1 cup water

zest of 3 limes

½ cup fresh lime juice

To make ice-cream: dissolve half the sugar in the water on low heat, then boil to thread stage. Pour onto egg yolks and beat with an electric mixer on high for about 10 minutes until thick and very pale and quite cool. Mix remaining sugar and lime juice into mango puree. Fold mango and cream into egg mix, churn in an ice-cream machine and freeze. Alternatively, freeze for 3 hours, rebeat and return to freezer. The ice-cream needs to be in the freezer for at least 8 hours before serving.

To make lime syrup: combine sugar and water in a saucepan and simmer together, cooking for approximately 10 minutes so that a syrupy texture is achieved — ideally the volume would reduce by half. Grate lime zest finely. Remove syrup from heat and add juice and zest. Chill and serve over mango ice-cream.

*The sugar syrup for the ice-cream needs to be boiled to 'thread stage' which literally means that the syrup will hold a thread when drizzled from a teaspoon. Sugar syrup is incredibly hot and will give a nasty burn, so be careful. For the lime syrup, instead of grated zest you can use strips of zest, but be sure to blanch them before adding to the syrup.*

# shortbread biscuits

makes 24 biscuits

1½ cups plain flour

1 heaped tablespoon self-raising flour

2 heaped tablespoons rice flour

2 tablespoons caster sugar,
plus extra to finish

180 g cold butter

Preheat oven to 140°C. Sift all dry ingredients together. Cut butter into small pieces and quickly rub into dry ingredients with your fingertips until the mixture is crumbly. Knead and flatten into a square about 1 cm high. Cut into rectangles, about 5 cm x 3 cm. Prick with a fork and sprinkle lightly with caster sugar. Place onto a baking sheet with a metal spatula and bake for 50 minutes. Cool and store in an airtight tin for up to 1 month.

*Possibly my most favourite biscuits. My mum makes these, my grandmother makes these, my aunty makes these … they're so buttery and the rice flour gives them a fabulous texture.*

# Glacé quince and pistachio biscotti

makes 40 small biscuits

125 g whole almonds (skin on)

2¾ cups plain flour

1⅔ cups sugar

½ teaspoon baking powder

1 teaspoon fennel seeds

125 g raw shelled pistachios

3 large eggs

3 egg yolks

1 teaspoon each lemon, lime, orange zest

1 teaspoon vanilla essence

125 g diced glacé quince

Preheat oven to 180ºC. Roughly chop almonds. Mix all dry ingredients in an electric mixer using the paddle attachment. Beat eggs and egg yolks in a separate bowl until mixed. Add eggs, zest, vanilla and quince to the mixer and mix with dry ingredients on a slow speed to form a dough. Divide the dough into 3 logs, approximately 25 cm x 5 cm, place on a floured tray and bake for about 20 minutes or until lightly coloured. Cool. Slice each log on an angle to produce individual biscuits. Lie the biscuits flat on the tray and bake again until dry, about another 20 minutes. Cool and store in an airtight tin for up to 1 month.

*These very crunchy, double-cooked biscuits are terrific dipped in sabayon, crème brûlée and with short blacks.*
*You can use glacé pear or orange if quince is unavailable.*

# Lemon curd

makes 3 cups

230 g unsalted butter
460 g caster sugar
5 eggs, beaten
¾ cup fresh lemon juice

Melt butter and sugar together in a bowl over a pot of simmering water. Whisk in eggs and lemon juice, stirring constantly. Cook over medium heat, stirring occasionally, until mixture coats the back of a spoon, about 15 minutes. Cool. Will keep refrigerated for 1 week.

Serve with meringues or in trifle.

# Apricot sauce

makes 3 cups

250 g dried Australian apricots
3½ cups water
⅓ cup lemon juice
875 g sugar

Soak apricots overnight in the water. Slowly bring to the boil and then simmer gently until tender and pulpy. Add lemon juice and sugar. Stir constantly until dissolved. Blend with a hand held mixer or in a food processor — be careful as it will be very hot. Leave to cool slightly before bottling in sterilised jars. Keeps for 3 months.

Serve drizzled over vanilla ice-cream scattered with praline (recipe page 110).

*basics, extras,*
*bits and pieces*

# To bone a bird

The aim when boning a bird is to keep as much meat attached to the skin, and as little meat on the bones, as you can.

Start with the bird breast side up. Cut off the wing tip and next joint. Pop the leg joints from their sockets. Place the bird breast side down. Using a boning or small knife cut along the centre of the back through the skin to the bone, going around the parson's nose in a V.

Work down one side separating the flesh from the bones. Cut through the soft cartilage to separate the wing from the carcass. As you move along the back you will notice the 'oyster' sitting in the back, be sure to cut that out rather than leave it on the bones. As you work towards the breast ensure that you remove the tenderloin with the flesh.

Cut through the leg joint where it is attached to the back and carry on cutting, always as close to the bone as you can, to detach the flesh from the rib cage. Once you reach the top of the breastbone, start from the other side and work down using the same method, cutting and scraping the flesh from the carcass.

You will reach a point where the carcass will be connected to the flesh only at the very top of the breast. Cut the carcass away from the flesh. You will now have a flat bird with wing and leg bones. With the point of the knife, tunnel around each wing bone to remove. Cut around the thigh bone and remove. Pull the drumstick up and away from the skin and cut the flesh from around the bone. You will need to cut out the fine bones and tendons in the leg area.

Lay the bird flat and even out the flesh in the legs. Take the tenderloins and use them to fill the space in between the breast. The bird is now ready to be stuffed.

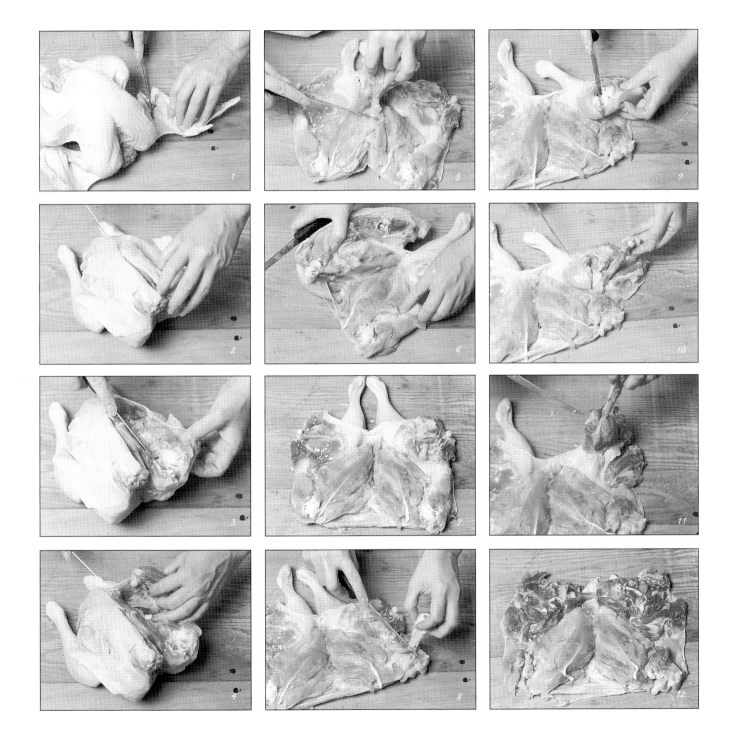

# chicken stock

3 chicken carcasses

2 carrots

1 celery stick

1 brown onion

1 bulb garlic

¼ cup olive oil

1 cup white wine

6 peppercorns

10 parsley stalks

6 fresh thyme stalks

Preheat oven to 140°C. Roughly chop vegetables. Roast carcasses and vegetables in a baking tray with olive oil until browned. Tip into stockpot. Place the baking tray on top of stove and add wine. Reduce the wine by half over medium heat. Scrape any meat and vegetables from the bottom of the baking tray and add them and the reduced wine to stockpot with herbs and peppercorns. Cover with cold water and bring to boil. Skim regularly. At boiling point turn heat down and simmer for 2–3 hours. Strain, discard vegetables and carcasses. Cool. Keeps for 2–3 days in the fridge, or frozen for up to a month.

# Fish stock

2 fish heads

2 carrots

1 celery stick

1 brown onion

1 bulb garlic

¼ cup olive oil

2 fish carcasses

6 parsley stalks

6 peppercorns

slice lemon rind

1 cup white wine

Remove the eyes and gills from the heads. Roughly chop vegetables. In a large stockpot sauté vegetables in oil for 10 minutes over low heat. Add fish heads and carcasses, parsley stalks, peppercorns and lemon rind and turn heat to high. Add white wine and reduce for a couple of minutes. Cover with cold water and bring to the boil. Skim regularly. At boiling point, turn heat down and simmer gently for 30 minutes. Strain, discard vegetables and fish. Cool. Keeps for 2–3 days in the fridge, or frozen for up to a month.

# Praline

200 g sugar

4 tablespoons water

150 g almonds

Preheat oven to 180°C. Roast almonds until aromatic and toasted, about 5 minutes. Boil sugar and water together. Just as the syrup turns golden, add almonds. Mix with a wooden spoon and pour onto an oiled tray. This is incredibly hot and will continue to cook after it is taken off the heat. Cool to room temperature — do not refrigerate. The praline will go brittle and quite hard. With a mortar and pestle or in a food processor crush the praline. I like to leave some chunky and let some go to a powder.

# Caramelised onion

10 medium brown onions

4 tablespoons honey

½ cup olive oil

salt and pepper, to season

2 tablespoons balsamic vinegar

Preheat oven to 150°C. Peel onions and slice thinly. Put into a baking tray and drizzle with honey and olive oil. Cover the tray with foil and bake for 45 minutes. Remove foil, stir and cook for a further 15 minutes or until dark and caramelised. Season and stir in balsamic vinegar.

Caramelised onion will keep in the fridge for up to 2 weeks.

# Roasted tomatoes

3 stalks parsley

½ cup chives (1 bunch)

½ cup fresh thyme

½ cup fresh oregano

12 tomatoes

salt and pepper, to season

olive oil

Preheat over to 160ºC. Lay half the herbs on a steel tray. Core tomatoes and cut in half. Place cut side up over the herbs. Sprinkle with salt and pepper and drizzle with olive oil. Cover with rest of herbs and cook for 40–60 minutes until about half original size.

Roasted tomatoes keep well for 4–5 days in the fridge.

# Salsa verde

½ cup fresh thyme

1 cup flat-leaf parsley

½ cup chives (1 bunch)

1 stalk rosemary

1 clove garlic

¼ cup red wine vinegar

2 anchovies

1 tablespoon capers (rinsed of salt)

1 teaspoon cracked black pepper

1 cup olive oil

Remove herbs from stalks and roughly chop. Mince garlic. Pulse in food processor with vinegar, anchovies, capers and cracked pepper. Drizzle in oil.

Salsa verde is best when used within a couple of hours, but will keep in the fridge for a couple of days.

# Basic mayonnaise

makes 1½ cups

1 egg yolk

½ teaspoon of salt

½ teaspoon pepper

2 tablespoons lemon juice

1 cup olive oil

By hand or in a food processor whisk yolk with seasoning and lemon juice. Gradually drizzle in the oil, whisking continuously until oil is incorporated. Taste — you may need more salt. This recipe can also be used as a base for any flavoured mayonnaise.

# Aioli

makes 1½ cups

1 bulb garlic

1 tablespoon olive oil

salt and pepper, to season

3 sprigs fresh thyme

1½ cups basic mayonnaise

1 teaspoon Dijon mustard

Preheat over to 150ºC. On a square of aluminium foil place unpeeled garlic. Drizzle with oil and season. Add thyme and fold up loosely like a parcel. Roast for 35 minutes or until soft. Cool — the garlic will be extremely hot inside its skin. Remove skin and mash roasted garlic. Fold garlic and mustard into mayonnaise.

# Basil and walnut pesto

makes 1 cup

½ cup walnuts

4 cloves garlic

2 cups basil leaves

¼ cup grated parmesan

1 cup olive oil

salt and pepper, to season

Preheat oven to 180ºC. Roast walnuts until aromatic and toasted, about 5 minutes. While still warm, rub the skins off as best you can (I find rubbing them in a folded tea towel works best). Crush garlic to paste, and process in a food processor with basil, walnuts and parmesan. Drizzle oil into mixture while the motor is still running. Season to taste.

# Rocket pesto

makes 1 cup

3 cups rocket

6 cloves garlic

¼ cup pine nuts

¼ cup grated parmesan

1 cup fruity olive oil

Blanch rocket in a pot of boiling water for 10 seconds, then refresh by plunging into cold water. Wring out and chop finely. Crush garlic to a paste. Process rocket, garlic, nuts and parmesan in a food processor. Drizzle oil into mixture while the motor is still running. Add more or less oil, depending on the consistency required.

# Flatbread

makes 12 large pieces

450 g plain flour

1 teaspoon salt

¾ cup milk

1 teaspoon sugar

2 teaspoons dried yeast

50 g melted butter

2 tablespoons plain yoghurt

robust flavoured olive oil, to cook and serve

sea salt, to cook and serve

Mix all ingredients together to form a dough. Knead for 5 minutes on a floured bench. The dough will become smooth and quite elastic. Leave as 1 piece; brush the outside with oil, cover with a damp cloth and leave to prove in a warm place for a couple of hours. The dough should approximately double in size. Knock back by pounding the risen dough so that it deflates, and knead for a further 30 seconds. Divide dough into 12 pieces. Using your hands, shape and stretch the dough into circles about 15 cm in diameter. Brush with oil and sprinkle with sea salt. Leave for about 15 minutes so they begin to rise again. Have the barbecue plate or a flat pan hot, slap the flatbread down and cook for about 1 minute. Turn over and brown the other side.

Serve hot drizzled with olive oil and some extra sea salt, if desired.

*Flatbread is so easy to prepare and so yummy that you'll start eating it before you can serve it. Be generous with the sea salt and use piquant olive oil.*

# Crunchy toasts

makes about 36 pieces

1 baguette

salt and pepper, to season

olive oil, to drizzle

Preheat oven to 180°C. Slice bread as thinly as you can. Place slices in a single layer on a baking tray, season generously with sea salt and freshly ground pepper and drizzle with olive oil. Bake until golden, about 10 minutes. Cool and store in an airtight container for up to 2 weeks.

These delicious and versatile toasts keep well and beat hands down any packaged toast or biscuits.

# Basil toasts

makes about 36 pieces

1 baguette or ciabatta loaf

¾ cup basil and walnut pesto

(recipe page 113)

Preheat oven to 170°C. Slice the bread thinly, preferably on the diagonal, and lay on a baking tray. Brush or spread pesto thinly on bread and bake until crisp, about 10 minutes. Cool and store in an airtight container for up to 2 weeks.

# Menus

# Relaxed autumn dinner

*The first sign that the long hot summer is over seems to be the chill in the air that haunts early evening. This menu has both a touch of sophistication and a casual feel of simplicity that means you will be with your guests, not in the kitchen!*

seared scallop salsa

hiramasa carpaccio

ricotta gnocchi with pancetta and cabernet vinegar

braised lamb with endamame salad

pavlova roll with passionfruit cream

# Christmas lunch

*My family always share a meal at Christmas. Great food, loads of goodwill, excited children and a sleep in the afternoon is Christmas for me.*

scallop and smoked salmon lasagne

turkey with Mediterranean stuffing

snap pea salad

caramelised pumpkin and shallots

liqueur fruits semi-freddo

# Gourmet barbecue

*Barbecues are so sophisticated these days, it's no longer chopped wood and a torch out on the back lawn! An all-weather appliance, it seems my barbecue at home is almost my kitchen now.*

avocado crostini

my favourite marinated beef

crayfish tails

potato, asparagus and pea salad

wilted cucumber salad

tomatoes with basil and cream

summer pudding

# Beach brunch

*I always think of thirst, hunger and salty lips after a couple of hours at the beach. Easy, tasty food you can snack on all day is the go. The cake is especially good as its crumbly moist texture fills even the most famished tummies.*

hommus with basil toasts

cold mushroom risotto bites

lamb koftas

asparagus and wild rice salad

plum and polenta cake

# Casual drinks

*For drinks, I try to make food that is small yet substantial, and full of flavour so that you always want another piece. It's also important to have a variety of tastes to tempt all your guests.*

grilled parmesan polenta

eggplant jam and flatbread

tuna tartare

prawn and paprika pancakes

mushroom risotto bites

salmon gravlax

shortbread biscuits

# Family lunch

*This whole salmon is such a great dish to serve buffet style. At our family lunches everyone wants to sit and eat, drink wine and talk for hours, constantly going back for just a little bit more. We usually end up eating pudding for dinner!*

eggplant jam and flatbread

pumpkin and prosciutto stuffed turkey

whole baked salmon with lentil sauce

rocket salad

Greek salad with Yarra Valley fetta

chocolate tart

# summer dinner

*Balmy nights, cool salads and fresh fish are the essence of our summer lifestyle. This is a combination that works every time. Marinated olives and cold champagne are a good way to kick off the evening.*

yabbie salad

snapper with Indian spiced potatoes

mango ice-cream and lime syrup

# Luxurious meal

*Cooking for friends on a special occasion is a privilege for them and you. Luxurious food doesn't need to be difficult or fussy though, the trick is to use the very best of everything you can find (or afford!).*

crab pasta

crispy roasted spatchcock

grilled figs with chilled sabayon

glacé quince and pistachio biscotti

# Vegetarian flavours

*A luscious combination of fresh, simple tastes.*
*The disarming richness of the white chocolate mousse wraps up a delicious, otherwise light, dinner.*

grilled parmesan polenta

field mushroom and rocket salad

pasta with olives and herbs

white chocolate mousse with poached strawberries

# Food to give

*There's something about the extra effort involved when you give gifts you've made yourself, they're bound to be well*
*received. It's hard to go wrong with these — they're all simple to make, look good and taste great.*

shortbread biscuits

glacé quince and pistachio biscotti

apricot sauce

hommus

lemon curd

# Inspirations

I read a lot of cookbooks and talk food and recipes continuously with fellow cooks, customers, family and friends. Many of these recipes have grown and developed over time and discussion. The following books have been of particular inspiration:

*From Tapas to Meze* Joanne Weir, Crown Publishing Group, 1994.

*The Dean & Deluca Cookbook* Dean and Deluca Rosengarten, Elbury Press, 1997.

*My Food* Chong Liew and Elizabeth Ho, Allen and Unwin, 1995.

*Sugar Club Cookbook* Peter Gordon, Hodder Headline, 1998.

# Kate Lamont

Kate Lamont lived in the Swan Valley just outside Perth for the first thirty years of her life. She discovered a passion for cooking while pursuing a career as a winemaker. In the mid-eighties, with the support of their parents, Kate and her sister Fiona opened a restaurant at Lamonts Winery. With the emphasis on fresh, simple, regional food, the restaurant has proved a great and enduring success. In the mid-nineties, Kate and Fiona opened a Lamonts' outlet in Perth focussing on fine produce, catering, take out and hampers. Most recently, Kate has opened a restaurant in East Perth. Already established as one of Perth's premier restaurants, it has cemented Lamonts' position in the forefront of the local food scene. Kate's love of cooking and entertaining are at the very heart of her success.

# Index